ANCIENT WARRIORS

VIKINGS

KENNY ABDO

Fly!
An Imprint of Abdo Zoom
abdobooks.com

abdobooks.com

Published by Abdo Zoom, a division of ABDO, P.O. Box 398166, Minneapolis, Minnesota 55439.

Printed in the United States of America, North Mankato, Minnesota.
102020
012021

Photo Credits: Alamy, Icon Sportswire, iStock, North Wind Picture Archives, Shutterstock
Production Contributors: Kenny Abdo, Jennie Forsberg, Grace Hansen
Design Contributors: Dorothy Toth, Neil Klinepier, Laura Graphenteen

Library of Congress Control Number: 2019956157

Publisher's Cataloging-in-Publication Data

Names: Abdo, Kenny, author.
Title: Vikings / by Kenny Abdo
Description: Minneapolis, Minnesota : Abdo Zoom, 2021 | Series: Ancient warriors | Includes online resources and index.
Identifiers: ISBN 9781098221270 (lib. bdg.) | ISBN 9781098222253 (ebook) | ISBN 9781098222741 (Read-to-Me ebook)
Subjects: LCSH: Vikings--Juvenile literature. | Scandinavia--Juvenile literature. | Discovery and exploration, Norse--Juvenile literature. | Civilization--Juvenile literature. | Military art and science--Juvenile literature. | Soldiers--Juvenile literature.
Classification: DDC 948.022--dc23

TABLE OF CONTENTS

VIKINGS

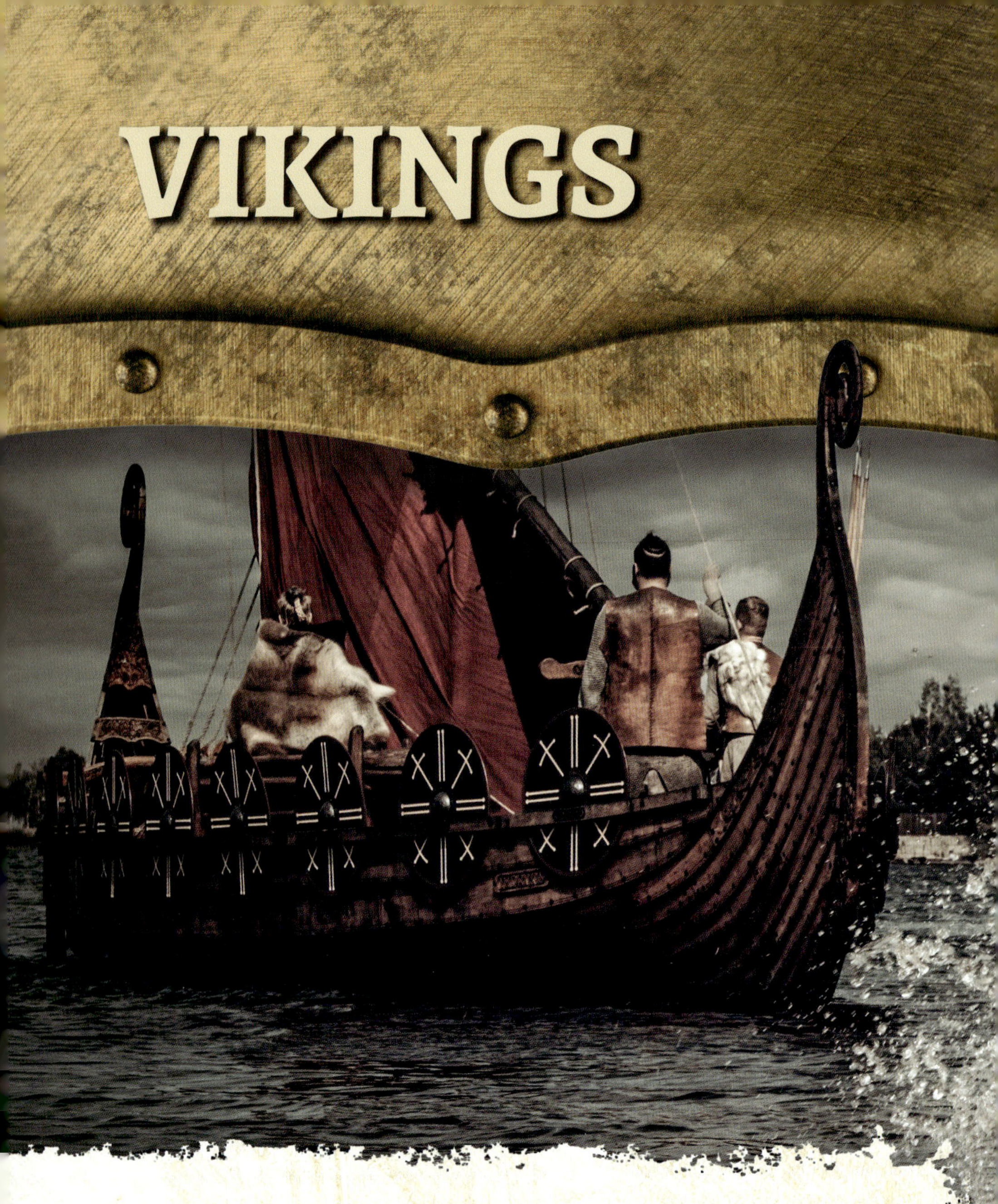

Raiding and **colonizing** throughout Europe, Vikings took what they wanted when they wanted it.

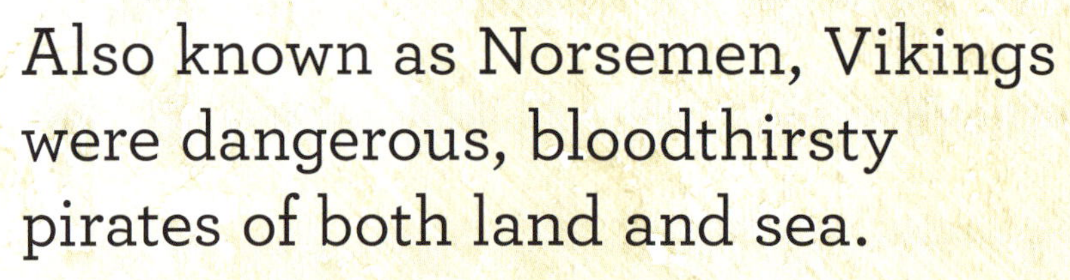

Also known as Norsemen, Vikings were dangerous, bloodthirsty pirates of both land and sea.

THE WARRIORS

The word “viking” comes from the Old Norse word *víkingr*. It was used to describe someone who went on **expeditions** by sea. Later, the word described a bad-natured pirate.

50
100
150 mi
NORWEGIAN SEA
Trondheim
Ålesund
Vaasa
FINLAND
Gulf of Bothnia
NORWAY
Aland Islands (FIN.)
HELSINKI
OSLO
Gulf of Finland
SWEDEN
Fredrikstad
STOCKHOLM
TALLINN
Hiiumaa (EST.)
ESTONIA
Vänern
Kristiansand
Saaremaa (EST.)
Skagerrak
Gulf of Riga
Göteborg
Frederikshavn
Kattegat
Gotland (SWE.)
SEA
LATVIA
RIGA
DENMARK
Öland (SWE.)
BALTIC SEA
Helsingborg
COPENHAGEN
Malmö
LITHUANIA
Bornholm (DEN.)
VILNIUS
Kaliningrad
RUSSIA
Kiel
Gdańsk
Rostock
Hamburg
Bremerhaven
Bremen
BE
Hannover
POLAND
BERLIN
Poznań
WARSAW
GERMANY
Łódź
Leipzig
Dresden
Lublin
Frankfurt
UK

Vikings lived in northern Europe during the **Middle Ages**. Most came from lands that are Norway, Denmark, and Sweden today.

At home, Vikings were mainly farmers. At sea they were fierce **pillagers**. Historians believe they did this because of **overpopulation** at home.

WARFARE & TACTICS

The Vikings would board their ships and head across the water. They would trade with or raid villages on islands such as Great Britain and its regions England, Scotland, and Wales.

Longships were narrow and designed for speed. Vikings also built cargo ships called *knarr* for trading. These were wider and deeper, and could fit more supplies than longships.

Vikings would use swords, lances, and spears. Some used a two-handed axe in battle that could easily cut through metal.

The power-hungry Vikings often battled kings. The Battle of Tettenhall took place in 910 CE. They fought an **Anglo-Saxon** army in a battle for land. The Vikings killed three kings and thousands of others in the process.

In 1066, the Vikings, led by King Harald Hardrada of Norway were defeated by the English and King Harold Godwinson. This defeat forced the Vikings to stop growing their territory. They also slowly stopped raiding other lands.

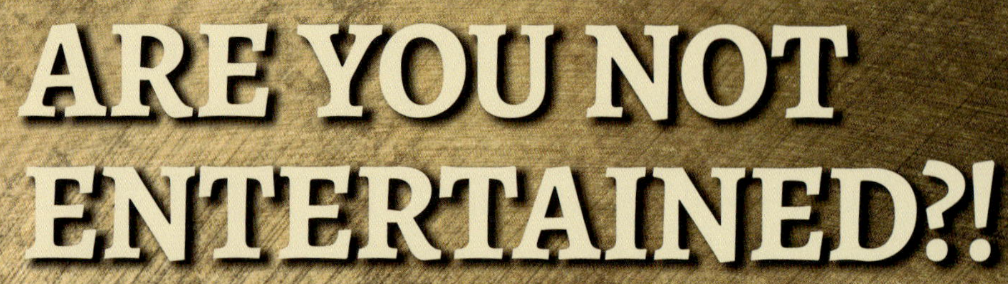

ARE YOU NOT ENTERTAINED?!

The Vikings left their mark on history and in today's society. Minnesota's NFL team is named after them. Many places **colonized** by the Vikings still stand today, like Dublin, Ireland.

Fortunately, the lifestyle of the Viking declined during the 11th century. So, nobody will see them coming ashore, ready to **pillage**.

GLOSSARY

Anglo-Saxon – a group of people of German descent who lived in Great Britain during the 5th century.

colonize – to establish settlement in a certain place and take control of it.

expedition – a planned out journey taken by a group of people.

Middle Ages – the period of European history between ancient time and the Renaissance, from 476 to 1453 CE.

overpopulation – when a certain place is populated with too many people.

pillage – to forcefully take goods from a place.

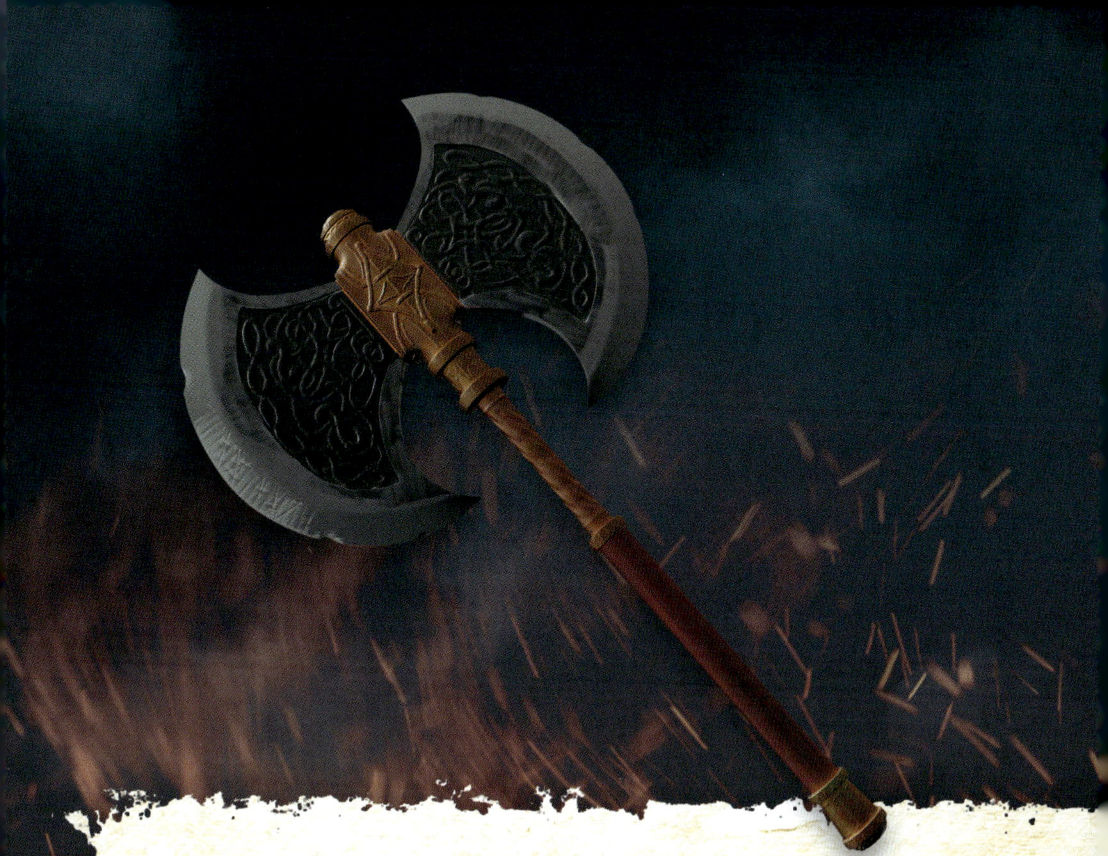

ONLINE RESOURCES

To learn more about Vikings, please visit **abdobooklinks.com** or scan this QR code. These links are routinely monitored and updated to provide the most current information available.

INDEX